For everyone.

It's your reflection.

What do you want it to do?

our Yorrim book

Look inside the mirror,

See that person there?

Are they happy, perky, peppy,

Or do they glare and stare?

If you sit still,
Do they move and squawk?
Or do they just watch,
Yawn, pout and gawk?

Could you reach right in,
And tickle about?
To make them laugh,
Giggle and shout?

If you want your pal to smile,
You could be there for quite a while!
You see, even when it's very late,
Your friend in the mirror can wait and wait!

But what if you could
Make them grin,
By popping a smile
On top your chin?!

"A-choo!"

See, here's a secret not well known,
The mirror only copies what it's shown.
That's just how it works my friend,
And on this much you can depend.

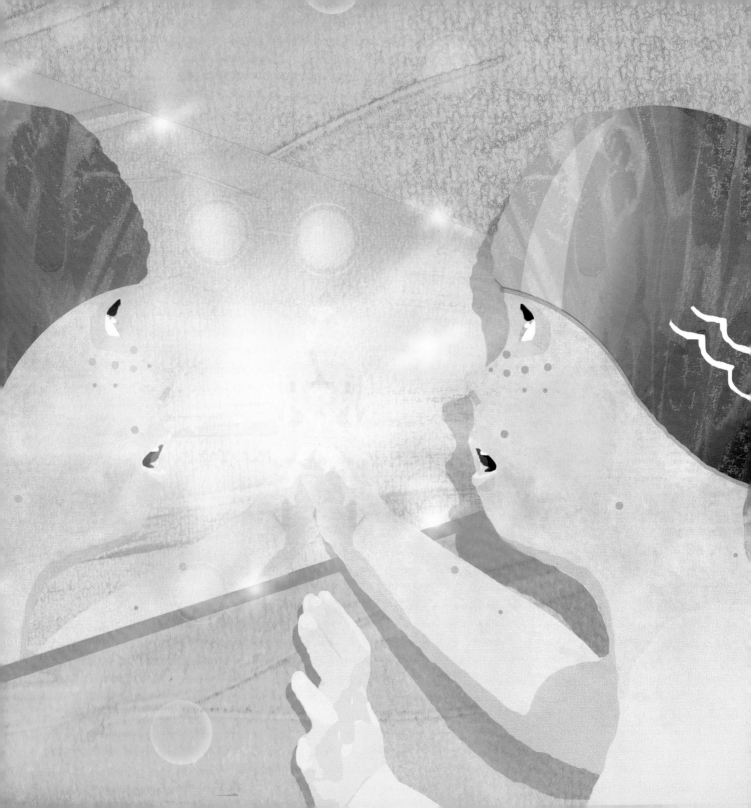

...But here's the biggest secret yet.
It's super special, so get set!

The whole world
Is a mirror too!
And that's something true,
For you, and you,
...And even you!

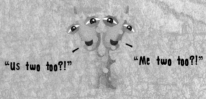

"Us two too?!"   "Me two too?!"

See, life reflects
What you put out,
Whether you sing and smile,
Or sulk and pout!

Smile long enough,
And smiles come back.
It's pretty fun,
Give it a crack!

But if you flip this upside down,

You could just sport a big ol' frown.

See, it's not your fault, what you go through,

But how you look at things is up to you!

Hard things
still happen
to good people!

But changing your face
Is just the start.

...Bigger smiles come Straight from your heart!

So if LOVE is the thing
You choose to do,
Then the people you meet
Will love you too!

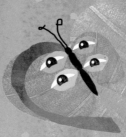

See, if you feel
Love for all creatures,
The world reflects
Its wildest features!

And if you believe
That people are kind,
That's a reflection
You'll start to find.

For to those who wonder
What might be...

Come wonders from
The sky and sea.

So if you tell yourself
That you can do it,
The world will show you
There's nothing to it.

But if you say
"I can't, no way,"
The world will obey
Just what you say.

So change it to
"I haven't done it ...YET!"
And pretty soon you will,
You can bet!

So when you talk to yourself,
Please keep in mind,
To make sure you say it very kind.
And tell the mirror 'I love you' every day,
Then the world can show you
It's all YAY!!

The reflections you'll see
Can be something new.

And the fun part is,
They start in you!

Hi. I'm Alex Wallman. I live in California, and this is my first book!

This book explores the idea that what we put out is what we get back!

So keep doing what you love until the mirrors in your life begin bouncing back awesomeness! And if you do something new and don't see your reflections change right away, don't give up! Just do what you love, because you love to do it, and good things will happen!

If you'd like to say hi, or find out about other fun new things, please visit www.alexwallman.com or email alex.author.man@gmail.com.

Thank you Ana Calderon, Devendra Banhart, Tim Nordwind, Jonny Pierce, Sam Wallman, Beck Wallman, Diane Wallman, Richard Wallman, David Hache, Field Garthwaite, Juan Palacio, Felicia Rangel, Joaquín Brown, Gabby Rangel, Darryl Anka, Simon Dargan, Dan & Charlie Calderon, Hannah Wood, Mike Edge, Tita Poe, Jessica Lipman, Carole Shipley, Pedro & Cheryl Calderon, Colin Donahue, Jackie Van Vught, Leah Anderson, Ron Anderson, Melissa Troedel, James Oliver, Harley Ridgway, Richie Edelson, Nico Edelson, Dimitri Kalagas, Calliope Edelson, Frances Webb, Chris Holmes, Jessica Reardon, Andrew Neuhues, Thomas Becker, Henry Shaw, Ben Woodward, Agustine Roelofs, Clare Hollander, Brent Pearson, Ethan Delorenzo, Haven Howel, John Saba, Candice Dragonas, Chris Cork, Frances Vanwyngarden, Dallas Clayton, Megan Myers, Ashby Myers, Scout Willis, Andrew Redpath, Jay Rifkin, John Kassab, Janell Shirtcliff, Rob Kolar, Galen Pehrson, Kinsa and Luna.

www.alexwallman.com

LCCN: 2016931954

ISBN: 9780692468579

10 9 8 7 6 5 4 3 2 1

Published by Rokeby House in Los Angeles, California.

Written and illustrated by Alex Wallman.

Enjoy! Pass it on to a friend. Be good to animals. And tell your mom you love her.

Printed by Friesens', an FSC® certified printer, utilizing part post-consumer waste.

Friesen's is an employee-owned company that uses 100% renewable energy and vegetable-based inks.

Printed in Canada.